T
VAMPIRE
AND
99
OTHER
HOWL-OWEEN
RIDDLES

by Ferida Wolff and Dolores Kozielski
illustrated by Chris Reed

Scholastic Inc.

New York Toronto London Auckland Sydney
Mexico City New Delhi Hong Kong Buenos Aires

No part of this publication may be reproduced in whole or in part, or
stored in a retrieval system, or transmitted in any form or by any
means, electronic, mechanical, photocopying, recording, or
otherwise, without written permission of the publisher. For
information regarding permission, write to Scholastic Inc.,
Attention: Permissions Department,
557 Broadway, New York, NY 10012.

ISBN 0-590-12028-X

Text copyright © 1992 by Ferida Wolff and Dolores Kozielski.
Illustrations copyright © 1992 by Chris Reed. All rights reserved.
Published by Scholastic Inc., 557 Broadway, New York, NY 10012.
SCHOLASTIC and associated logos are trademarks and/or registered
trademarks of Scholastic Inc.

12 11 10 9 8   3 4 5 6 7/0

Printed in the U.S.A.   01

For my father, Sam Mevorach
FW

For Jim, Andrea, and Michael
DK

We'd like to thank

Debbie Barr
Tara Hrivnak
Theresa Hrivnak
Kathy Joynes
Elizabeth Ann Livingston
Jessica Lynch
Dan McNamara
Carolyn Peluso
Christine Marie Peluso
Beth Thompson
Allison Venuto

for listening and laughing.

CONTENTS

S C A R E
YOURSELF
S I L L Y !

Are you afraid of ghosts? Do skeletons send you scurrying into the closet to hide? Do you have a coffin fit every time you think of vampires? When you read this collection of frightfully funny riddles, you'll have a howling good time. Find out what mother ghosts read to baby ghosts, what werewolves sing at railroad stations, and much more. Halloween comes once a year, but these riddles will keep you laughing all year long!

COUNT DRACULA

What do you get when you cross Dracula
with anything?

You get Dracula very angry.

Why is Dracula good at math?

Because when he was little his mother
made him Count

How did the vampire get a sore throat?

From her coffin

Is there any difference between 16
ounces of hamburger and finishing
off Dracula?

No. They're both a pound of stake.

What does a polite vampire send
to her victim?

A fang-you note

How does Dracula decorate his house
for Halloween?

With black and orange cape paper

What does Dracula use for bait when he
goes fishing?

Bloodworms

Why did the vampire go to the library?
He wanted to get a book he could sink his
teeth into.

**Why shouldn't you tell your troubles
to a vampire?**
Because he will give bat advice

What do you call twin boy vampires?

Blood brothers

What did Dracula put on top of his barn roof?

A weather vein

What's the difference between the sting of a black widow and Dracula's soda?

One is a spider's bite, the other is a biter's Sprite.

What do traffic signs in Transylvania say?

Fly and Don't Fly

What's worse than a bald werewolf?

A toothless vampire

Why does Dracula go bowling in the evening?

Because he only strikes at night

Why is it hard to be Dracula's friend?

Because he can be very draining

Why did the vampire put vegetables in her coffin?

She wanted to rest in peas.

What did Dracula use to fix the kitchen sink?

Vampliers

WITCHES'
BREW

Why did the witch go to the doctor?
Because she was having dizzy spells

What did the witch get when she put a
toad in her pigpen?
Warthogs

What did the wizard do when he saw the
first star at night?
He made a witch.

**What noise do you hear at the witches'
racetrack?**

Brooom, brooom, brooooom

What sounds does a witch's cereal make?

Snap, cackle, pop

What did the witch receive for her
starring role in a horror movie?

An Academy Awart

What do you call a witch without
a broom?

A ground hag

Why couldn't the letter carrier deliver
mail to the witch's cottage?

Because she didn't have a zip toad

What's green, black, and yellow and has
a peel?

A witch eating a banana

What does a witch do when she's sleepy?

She takes a catnap.

Why does a witch know everybody's business?

Because she's nosey

What does a witch keep in her house for a snack?

Cottage cheese

If there were 13 people at the witch's New Year's Eve party, how come the witch got to eat all the cake?

Because at midnight the clock struck 12

Why didn't the witch take a bath?

Because she liked to cast smells

What happened to the blackbird when it flew over the witch's garden?

It was turned into a scared crow.

What does a witch use to call
her friends?

A touch-toad phone

13

GHOSTS
AND
GHOULS

Why did the ghost bring her bracelet to
the jeweler?

To have it engraved

Why couldn't the ghoul sell her house?

Because she was charging an arm and a leg

What do you get when you cross
a ghost and a skunk?

Invisible stink

**What did Mother Ghost read to
Baby Ghost?**

Scary tales

What do you call a chicken that haunts houses?

A poultry-geist

What is a ghost's favorite ice-cream flavor?

Boo-berry swirl

What did Grandma Ghost say to Baby Ghost?

"Gitchy, gitchy, boo!"

What did the ghost name his new motel?

Rest-Inn-Peace

What do the cheerleaders at Ghost Town High try to create?

Ghoul spirit

What kind of gum do ghosts chew?
Spirit-mint

Where does a ghoul board a plane?
At a scareport

What did the ghost buy at the bakery?
A sheet cake

What did Dr. Frankenstein use to reach
the top shelf in his laboratory?
His step-ghoul

Why was the ghost afraid to bring home his report card?

Because he had bad graves

What game has 5 ghouls on each team?
Casketball

Why couldn't the ghost ride the bus?
Because she didn't have exact chains

Where do ghouls go to learn their ABC's?
To the little red ghoulhouse

What did the little ghost look forward to being?
All groan up

Who wears a sheet and coonskin cap?
Daniel Booooone

How long can a ghoul hold his breath?

Until he runs out of scare

What did the ghost bring back from his vacation in Australia?

A boo-merang

What's the difference between an awesome ghost and a crazy monster who collects thread?

One is a cool spook and the other is a spool kook.

How do ghosts keep their babies safe in the car?

They put them in car sheets.

MONSTER
M A S H

If everyone knocks twice on Halloween
night, why shouldn't you open the door
when you hear just one knock?

Because the Knock Less Monster is at
the door

What do sea monsters eat for lunch?

Seanut butter and scaly sandwiches

Why did the monster go to the
optometrist?

To get new eye-eye-eyeglasses

What song do you sing at a two-headed monster's birthday party?

"Happy Birthday Two You"

**What happened to the girl who was
eaten by the cucumber monster?**

She got herself into a pickle.

**When does Cookie Monster buy
new clothes?**

When his old ones get too crumby

**Why did the mad scientist throw a
hot dog into the pigpen?**

Because she wanted to meet
Dr. Frank-in-Sty

**What bill does the monster pay
on Halloween?**

The electrick bill

Where does a monster buy hamburgers, fries, and a shake?

At Burger Thing

When is a good time to leave a monster's party?

Before it starts

Why did the monster get sick to her stomach?

Because she ate in a past food restaurant

Why did the monster go to Hollywood?

To become a movie scar

Why does the monster hate jokes?

Because they make him laugh his head off

**Why did the boy bring a monster home
from the store?**

Because his mother sent him out for a
dozen legs

Which monster flew a kite in the middle of a thunderstorm?

Benjamin Franklinstein

When monsters play Hide-and-Seek, who gets to be It?

Everyone!

What keeps following the sea monster?

The D monster

What did the monster say when she ate the minute hand off the clock?

"May I have seconds?"

How many cookies can a monster eat?

As many as he wants

ASSORTED
SCREAMS

Why did the spider get a ticket?

He was weaving through traffic.

Why did the bald man go into the
haunted house?

He wanted to have a hair-raising
experience.

What did the mummy tell his girlfriend?

"You are so beautiful tomb me."

How do werewolves greet each other?
"Howl do you do?"

Where did the skeleton go on
her vacation?

To Yellowbone National Park

What did the devil give his girlfriend
when he proposed?

A 2-carat demon

Why was the undertaker upset when she
buried someone in the wrong plot?

Because she made a grave mistake

What time is it when you're stuck on a highway full of boa constrictors?

Crush hour

What did the werewolf sing while
he waited at the train station for his
next victim?

"I've Been Lurking on the Railroad"

Why did the skeleton change his
laundry detergent?

He had ring around the collarbone.

Why can't the devil keep a job?

Because he's always getting fired

What is the difference between
a giant and a troll?

About 12 feet

Why did the Blob travel to
Mount Everest?

It wanted to go mountain sliming.

What keeps flies out of a
monster's house?

A scream door

What's the difference between someone
having a nightmare and a cow seeing
a ghost?

One has a scary dream, the other has a
dairy scream.

Who helped Cinderella get to the
Halloween ball?

Her scary godmother

What brand of coffee do
werewolves drink?

Maxwell Howls

Why doesn't a skeleton use a towel after taking a shower?

Because she always comes out bone dry

**What is bad luck when it crosses
your path, crosses your path,
crosses your path?**

A black caterpillar

What did the werewolf say when he
arrived at the Halloween party?

"Hair I am!"

Why did the skeleton join the army?

He wanted to be in the armed corpses.

What kind of music does the
monster band play?

Rock and troll

What is the difference between
a spider and a duck?

One has 2 feet of web and the other has
2 webbed feet.

How do you know when the devil is
hiding in your garage?

You can hear his horns.